BR DIESELS

VOL 1

BR DIESELS
VOL 1
classes 24-31, 40-46, 76 and 77 systemwide

MAURICE DART

HALSGROVE

First published in Great Britain in 2010

British Library Cataloguing-in-Publication Data
A CIP record for this title is available from the British Library

ISBN 978 1 84114 987 5

HALSGROVE
Halsgrove House,
Ryelands Industrial Estate,
Bagley Road, Wellington, Somerset TA21 9PZ
Tel: 01823 653777   Fax: 01823 216796
email: sales@halsgrove.com

Part of the Halsgrove group of companies.
Information on all Halsgrove titles is available at: www.halsgrove.com

Printed and bound in China by Toppan Leefung Printing Ltd

CONTENTS

THE MAURICE DART COLLECTION

Maurice Dart was born in Plymouth and, apart from a period in Gibraltar, he has lived in Devon and Cornwall for all of his life. His interest in railways was bred into him almost from birth and has stayed with him. He was educated at Sutton High School, Plymouth followed by Plymouth & Devonport Technical College and worked as a chemist in the China Clay industry for thirty-seven years. Through his work connections he gained an intimate knowledge of the Lee Moor Tramway and of China Clay railway operations by the main line railway companies. Following retirement he works as a volunteer on the Bodmin & Wenford Railway mainly in the shop or escorting visiting enthusiasts around the railway. He also acted as a guide for enthusiasts who wish to visit sidings that serve locations owned by Imerys Minerals.

Now in his eighties, from a boy Maurice Dart has travelled throughout much of southern Britain armed with a camera, taking photographs of all things railway. His collection, now numbering many thousands of images, has been the source of many small publications and has been used in countless magazines and journals. His books with Halsgrove, published under the Maurice Dart Collection banner, include *Images of Cornish Railways, Images of Plymouth and South Devon Railways, Images of Exeter and East Devon Railways, Images of Bristol, Somerset and Dorset Railways, Images of Wiltshire Railways, Images of Bristol Railways, Images of Hampshire and Isle of Wight Railways, Images of Industrial & Narrow Gauge Railways - Devon* and *Images of Industrial & Narrow Gauge Railways - Cornwall.*

BR Diesels Volume 1 is the first book published by Halsgrove using colour images from The Maurice Dart Collection. *BR Diesels Volume 2* will cover Small Shunters, Classes 33, 50–55, 71–74 and Hydraulics.

The author acknowledges the help of *The Allocation of BR Diesels & Electrics* by Roger Harris in the compilation of this book.

INTRODUCTION

I was introduced to the railway hobby in my early childhood and through the years the interest steadily developed, so naturally I am a dedicated steam loco fan. I commenced taking photographs of locomotives in August 1947 and as steam was replaced by modern traction I turned the camera more to railway infrastructure and to the industrial railway scene. In the 1960s I started to photograph a minimal number of the new locos which were mainly Western Region Diesel Hydraulics. My holiday railway trips tended to be to South Wales or Lancashire with occasional visits to the London area. However in the early 1970s I began to explore wider areas of the country and started seeing representatives of different types of diesel and electric locos. An interest in these slowly developed and I commenced recording some of them photographically. Gradually I covered all passenger and many of the non-passenger lines in the country. I have always been an 'engine spotter' so having missed many of the early diesel types I earnestly set about seeing all remaining locos. Whereas in the past I had visited many steam locomotive sheds, visits to diesel depots commenced which presented me with numerous opportunities for photography. With the popularity of certain classes of diesel loco it was suggested by this publisher that some albums featuring specific classes of locos were produced using some of my colour slides and prints. This does not purport to be a complete history nor show all variations of each type. The locos are depicted in numerical order. Many books are available detailing the history and technical details of all diesel and electric classes so this information is not contained herein. Most of the shots were taken at diesel depots or at stations with a few from moving trains. Some of the views may contain items of detail of interest to modellers and many depict scenes which are no longer possible to record. I hope that this selection of my personal photos will appeal to many other fellow enthusiasts.

CLASS 20 DIESEL LOCOMOTIVES

The 1000hp class 20s were designed to work freight trains in pairs coupled nose to nose so action shots of them taken from the front end are rare. Occasionally they would appear on passenger trains which were normally summer workings to holiday resorts. It was only in later years that they appeared in the West Country and Southern England when they worked some excursion and weed killing trains. In preservation, as with many other types their sphere of activity has widened considerably. A loco at a depot with no allocation quoted means the loco is at home. One engine, 20166 features strongly in this book. I make no excuse for including a good selection of shots of this engine as it was based on the Bodmin & Wenford Railway for many years. As I am a working volunteer on that line I was afforded chances of obtaining some unusual shots of it at work.

The yard at Crewe Works on 4 December 1977 contained Cardiff Canton's class 47 47089 and 20005 from Toton depot.

Partly in shadow rounding the curve from Oakenshaw Junction 20023 leads 20205 into Wakefield Kirkgate on 3 January 1975. Both locos were based at Tinsley.

During an Open Day at Tinsley depot on 27 April 1996 20042 was paired with 20188. Both had been withdrawn and sold to Pete Waterman.

Passing Derby station on 2 January 1975 are 20043 and 20072. Both were from Toton depot.

Grubby 20047 is at the north end of Toton depot on 16 October 1976.

On the West Anglia Gala Day on 29 September 1990 a special train waits to depart from Cambridge for Fen Drayton. The 'WEST ANGLIAN ENTERPRISE' is headed by Toton's 20047 and 20004. This day presented the opportunity to cover the branch lines to Fen Drayton and Middleton Towers.

How to photograph six locos of the same type at work on one shot. This happened as 'pure luck'. I had decided to spend an hour on Langley Mill station to hopefully photograph a few freight trains passing late afternoon on 5 July 1988. A very slow moving train hauled by four class 20s appeared in the distance on the Up Slow Goods line. As it was nearing the station a fast train hauled by a pair of class 20s appeared on the Up Goods line and it was apparent that the fast train would pass inside the other before either reached me. So despite both trains being a little distant I seized the opportunity to include all six locos in the shot. The train on the nearest line is headed by 20215 from Toton and 20188 which had been officially transferred from Toton to Eastfield in May but was obviously still around. The other train is in charge of 20063 + 20032 + 20055 + 20169 which were all Toton engines.

On 3 March 1975 Toton's 20071 and 20076 pass eastbound through Nottingham Midland.

On 3 March 1975 20076 and 20071 have passed the author at Nottingham and may be heading to the Worksop area.

Standing outside the south end of Toton depot on 16 October 1976 is 20081.

Visible on 8 January 1983 on the stabling point at Carstairs were four class 20s and a 47. Identifiable were Eastfield's 20085, Haymarket's 20222 and 47542 from Gateshead.

Running light engine westbound through Falkirk Grahamston on 26 August 1983 is 20086 from Eastfield. The loco is about to pass below a typical Scottish station footbridge.

On 7 September 1983 the same engine, 20086 was in Mossend yard.

A line of class 20s at Toton on 16 October 1976 contained 20090.

On 7 July 1989 the author was surprised to find Toton's 20218 and 20099 awaiting departure from Blackpool North on a passenger working.

In 1992 20110 from the South Devon Railway was scheduled to travel by rail to be a guest at the Diesel Gala weekend on the Bodmin & Wenford Railway. En route it was stabled at St.Blazey depot where the depot manager permitted no one to enter to see it. Luckily the author had contacts in the Goods yard and he was conducted from there into the Maintenance shed where the loco is seen on 18 September 1992. To its rear is 37669.

Viewed from the other side of the track inside St.Blazey on 18 September 1992 are 20110 and 37669.

After the Diesel Gala was over 20110 is outside the Workshop at Bodmin General on 22 September 1992. 0-6-0ST 'SWIFTSURE' peeps around the right side of the building. Parts of another saddle tank are on the ground.

On 4 October 1995 20110 was at home in the yard at Buckfastleigh on the South Devon Railway.

In the morning of 2 September 1983 Eastfield's 20114 was at Fort William marshalling the stock for the steam run to Mallaig.

After enjoying the steam run to Mallaig and back on 2 September 1983 the author walked out to Tom-Na-Faire depot where he was permitted to take photos provided he did not cross any track. Walkways between the lines gave this view of the depot with 20114 and Eastfield's smartly turned out 37112.

This is a close up view of 20114 stabled inside one of the small sheds at Tom-Na-Faire depot on 2 September 1983.

At the South Devon Railway at Buckfastleigh on 9 November 2003 the yard held 20118 named 'SALTBURN-BY-THE-SEA' along with 25901.

This is Perth station during the evening of 23 August 1984. On the left on a train of tank wagons are Motherwell's 20137 and 20124. In the centre is 27008 from Inverness with 47622 on the right, which was based at Cardiff Canton.

A scene from the preservation era has D8142 outside the shed at Llangollen on 30 July 1997.

The yard at Ayr depot on 5 June 1976 contained Eastfield's 20011 and 20146.

The same engine 20146 heads east, light, through Falkirk Grahamston on 26 August 1983.

Two trains, both headed by a pair of class 20s pass on the Goods lines at Chesterfield on 14 June 1983. Heading south on the left are 20160 and 20158. Approaching northbound on the right are 20147 and 20169. All four were based at Toton. Luck was again with the author as 20147 was one of the two remaining members of the class that he had not seen.

This is 20166 at Bodmin General on 16 August 1993 a couple of months following its arrival from Dollands Moor. Withdrawn by British Rail from Toton on 17 May 1991 it was purchased for use on the B & W R in September of that year. Before arrival it was hired to RFS Industries who numbered it 2015 and they sub-hired it to CTTG for Channel tunnel construction work. It was numbered 35 in their fleet. The engine is in RFS livery and carries its RFS and CTTG numbers. The loco was preparing to work the weekly evening freight train for Fitzgerald Lighting.

Having worked the freight train to Bodmin Parkway and exchanged wagons with a class 37, 20166 worked the empty wagons back to Bodmin General. It ran round them, took them out to Walker Lines and shunted them into the sidings. It is ready to return from Walker Lines to Bodmin General around 21.00 on 16 August 1993.

Repainted in dark green, red and white with a black underframe 20166 'RIVER FOWEY' is at Bodmin General on 25 July 1995. The idea followed Thornaby depot's naming of some of their class 20s after local rivers.

To celebrate the author's 65th birthday on 31 January 1997 a small party of friends travelled behind 20166 from Bodmin General to Boscarne Junction. The train is waiting at Bodmin General for all participants to board the GWR 'TOAD'.

After detraining passengers at Boscarne Junction on 31 January 1997 20166 prepares to uncouple and run round the Toad.

Having run round the Toad at Boscarne Junction on 31 January 1997 the crew are shutting 20166 down and securing it before joining the party to adjourn to the Borough Arms for lunch. This followed the tradition of crews working Wenford Bridge trains who sometimes stopped at Dunmere Crossing for the same purpose!

About 19.30 on the evening of 3 June 1998 20166 is coupling to the Fitzgerald freight train at Walker Lines siding. On the left is class 10 shunter D3452 with part of 50042 'TRIUMPH' visible behind it.

Shortly after the previous shot 20166 slowly inches the train over the reverse curves from Walker Lines sidings.

After arrival at Bodmin Parkway on 3 June 1998 20166 ran around its train. Then 37671 'TRE POL AND PEN' arrived from St.Blazey with empty wagons and placed them in the transfer siding. 20166 is preparing to back out with the loaded wagons which will be attached to 37671 for onward transit.

The shunting to exchange empty and loaded wagons at Bodmin Parkway was somewhat complex. This resulted in 20166 being sandwiched between them on 3 June 1998.

After 37671 departed from Bodmin Parkway with the loaded wagons on 3 June 1998 20166 brings the empties into the platform line where it will run round them ready to take them up the bank to Bodmin.

An 'Open Day' for families and friends held by EWS at St.Blazey depot on 31 August 2002 was attended by 20166 which is beneath the stabling canopy.

Locos at Toton on 16 October 1976 included 20174.

At Frodingham depot on 12 April 1992, still in service was Thornaby's 20185. A class 37s hides away inside the shed.

Outside The Railway Age at Crewe on 23 September 1995 were Pete Waterman's 20188 and class 25 5222 (25072).

At Ayr depot on 27 August 1988 was Eastfield's 20193.

The yard at the north end of Toton depot on 16 October 1976 held 20195 and 20090.

Photographed from a Retford to Sheffield train on 15 October 1989 Toton's 20196 and 20084 are climbing from Whisker Hill Junction to the Main line at Retford. The first loco carried the number 20308 for a period. The second loco has since been numbered RFS 2002, CTTG 31 and 20302.

Another class 20 was acquired by the Bodmin & Wenford Railway for use as a source of spares for 20166. 20197 was stored at the back of one of the sidings at Walker Lines for a period. After this it moved to the south end of the refuge siding outside Bodmin General where it was recorded on 25 May 2004. Whilst at this location it was nicknamed 'The temporary buffer stop'. It never moved under its own power at Bodmin.

Among locos stabled at Thornton Junction on 25 September 1982 are 20203, 20225 and 20227 all of which were from Haymarket depot.

This is a shot of Millerhill depot from a diverted passenger train on 25 October 1987. Visible are Haymarket's 08755, Eastfield's 20205, Stratford's 47357, a class 26 and another class 47.

In the yard at Ayr depot on 27 August 1988 are 20205 and 20199, both from Eastfield depot.

Also at Ayr depot on 27 August 1988 were Eastfield's 20211 and 20193.

On 19 November 1977 Tinsley depot was host to 20212.

55. On the damp evening of 2 June 1976 Haymarket's 20218 banks a heavy coal train northwards through Dunfermline Lower. A pair of class 20s was on the front of the train.

20218 and 20099 wait at Blackpool North with a return passenger working on 7 June 1989. Both locos were from Toton depot.

On 2 June 1976 20222 and 20184 power a heavy northbound coal train through Dunfermline Lower. The train was assisted in the rear by 20218. The sound created by three class 20s working hard was phenomenal. All three locos were based at Haymarket.

Alongside Haymarket depot on 6 September 1983 are 20225, 47407 from Gateshead depot and another class 47.

Passing Shenfield on a Nuclear Flask train on 17 July 2002 are DRS owned 20308 and 20306. These locos had been numbered 20187 and 20131.

On 18 August 1997 Hunslet-Barclay owned 20903 (ex 20083) tails the weed killing train through Stoke-on-Trent. This was one of the four class 20s which hauled the 'Train for Life' to Kosovo in September 1999.

CLASSES 24 and 25
DIESEL LOCOMOTIVES

Class 24s worked in many areas apart from the West Country, Southern England and South Wales. Later when in departmental use one class 24 reached Penzance. The class 25's sphere of operation was far more widespread.

CLASS 24s

On 3 July 1974 Crewe Diesel's 24052 stands alongside the back of the coal stage at the site of Croes Newydd shed, Wrexham. The water tank is prominent atop the coal stage.

Partly in shadow outside Birkenhead shed, now a diesel depot, on 1 July 1974 is Crewe Diesel's 24054. In August 1976 this loco was transferred to Departmental stock and renumbered to TDB 96008.

On 17 June 1978 24066 is in the yard at Doncaster Works. This loco was withdrawn from Haymarket depot in February 1976. After storage at Carlisle it was brought here and was scrapped two months after this photo was taken.

Arpley stabling point at Warrington held 24078 and 24052 on 6 July 1974. Both were allocated to Crewe Diesel depot.

This is the yard at Llangollen shed on 4 September 1993. Centrepiece is 24081 which had been withdrawn from Crewe Diesel. It was acquired for preservation by Steamport, Southport and later moved to this location. It now resides on the Gloucester & Warwickshire Railway. In the background is GWR 5700 class 0-6-0PT 7754 with class 08 shunter D3265 (08195) on the right, both wearing 'faces' for a 'Thomas' event.

The old Lochgorm Locomotive Works at Inverness was transformed to serve as a diesel depot. In front of one of the sections on 2 June 1976 are 24123 from Haymarket. This loco was withdrawn six weeks later. Centre is 47271 also from Haymarket. On the right is 26039.

This is the Permanent Way/Engineers depot yard at Reading on 23 March 1980 with TDB 968009 (ex 24142) resident.

On 5 June 1976 the yard at Glasgow Works (St.Rollox/Springburn) was host to LNER A4 class 4-6-2 60009 'UNION OF SOUTH AFRICA' which had called in for some attention. However, to the rear of the A4 was 25024 which appeared to be of some interest to two enthusiasts. This was not surprising as the loco had been withdrawn from Tinsley depot in January and stored at Barrow Hill depot for a couple of months before coming here for scrapping. This was not carried out until December.

It is afternoon on Sunday 10 October 1974 and 25041 was outside the steam shed, in use as a diesel depot, at Barrow. The engine was based at Kingmoor, Carlisle.

On the same day, 10 October 1974, Kingmoor's 25042 was stabled in front of 25041 at Barrow shed.

Two days later, 12 October 1974, 25043 was stabled at Lancaster. This engine had officially been transferred from Kingmoor to Longsight the previous month but apparently this had to occur.

On 4 January 1975 the Locomotive Club of Great Britain ran the Pennine Venture Railtour. The train hauled by 25043 and 25082 stopped at Grindleford for photography as depicted. Both engines were based at Longsight.

Three locos were present in the carriage sidings at Exeter St.Davids on 27 May 1978. On the left is Eastleigh's 33016. Centre is Laira's 25048. On the right is 08281which was based at Newton Abbot.

The stabling point at Ladywell, Preston held Longsight's 25054 on 5 January 1975.

On 6 January 1975 25061 from Longsight brings an eastbound coal train through Manchester Victoria.

At Gloucester Horton Road depot on 12 August 1972 were 5213 which became 25063, 5828 which became 31295 and 5227 which became 25077. These locos were all based at Bath Road, Bristol.

This view of Gloucester Horton Road depot on 12 August 1972 contains Landore's 1611 which became 47032, and Bath Road's 5227 (25077) and 5828 (31295).

The LCGB's Pennine Venturer Railtour on 4 January 1975 hauled by Longsight's 25082 and 25043 called at Sowerby Bridge for a photo stop. Note the snow ploughs fitted to the front loco.

Longsight's snow plough fitted 25082 awaits its next banking duty at Manchester Victoria on 6 January 1975.

Following restoration 5233 (25083) is at the platform at Brechin 4 August 2002.

Heading a westbound freight train through Hunts Cross on 25 August 1972 is 25101 which was allocated to the Liverpool Division.

On 25 April 1977 Longsight's 25102 is at Buxton depot.

A westbound freight rounds the curve at Warrington Arpley to enter the large marshalling yard on 9 July 1973. It is hauled by 5256 (25106) from Springs Branch. Another class 25 waits by the exit from the stabling point.

A freight train probably carrying salt heads west through Northwich on 3 July 1974 headed by Spring Branch depot's 25111.

Springs Branch's 25138 rests inside Northwich shed on 3 July 1974.

Exeter depot on 4 June 1972 held Newton Abbot's 3808 (08641) and Laira's 7509 which became 25159.

The small yard at Keith Junction was host to a short freight headed by 25172 on 9 June 1976. The engine was based at Haymarket.

This is the Holding sidings at Preston on 8 July 1974. On the left are 37174 and 37172 both Immingham engines. Centre is 25190 from Kingmoor.

In the yard at Burnley Central on 8 July 1974 is Longsight's 25197.

Laira's 25216 runs round a train of loaded 'Clay Hood' wagons at ECC Rocks Dryers, adjacent to Goonbarrow Junction on 5 August 1976.

On 5 August 1976 25216 from Laira sets off from Goonbarrow Junction with loaded 'Clay Hood' wagons for Fowey.

On 14 May 1978 25220 from Crewe Diesel is
on Bath Road depot outside the Works. The
bogie has been removed from one end and the
loco is supported on blocks and jacks.

This is Crewe Diesel's 25220 jacked up at Bath
Road viewed form the other end on 14 May
1978.

Crewe Diesel's 25222 was in the rolling stock sidings at Cricklewood depot on 24 June 1978.

Laira's 7573 (25223) brings loaded wagons from Plymstock cement works past the sites of Lucas Terrace Halt and Friary loco shed on 3 May 1973.

On 1 May 1977 25223 and 25217, both from Laira stand near the turntable at St.Blazey shed.

A line of class 20s which include 20225 and 20227 along with 25226 are at Thornton Junction on 25 September 1982. All of the engines were allocated to Haymarket.

Early evening on 5 July 1972 Laira's 7577 (25227) shunts Container-flats in Truro goods yard.

This is another shot of 7577 (25227) from Laira on Long Rock shed on 5 July 1972. Visible in the left distance is Laira's D1054 'WESTERN GOVERNOR'.

This is Exeter depot on 17 June 1973. On the left is 7577 (25227) now allocated to Bath Road. Partly visible is 6541 (33023) from Eastleigh. To its right are Laira's D1034 'WESTERN DRAGOON' and 1683 (47485) from Bescot. Immediately behind the class 47 is 5202 (25052) from Springs Branch depot.

On 6 January 1975 Longsight's 25244 takes a van train eastwards through Manchester Victoria. This engine is preserved and has been at Swanage, Wansford and Tenterden.

Two Bescot engines, 25262 and 25253 are stabled at Wolverhampton on 22 April 1978.

On 3 July 1974 25279 from Springs Branch is on the fuelling apron at Northwich shed. This engine is preserved and has resided at Llangollen, Toddington, Northampton and Loughborough.

Here is 25279 numbered
D7629 at Llangollen shed on 4
September 1993.

In torrential rain D7629 stands
in the yard at Ruddington on
22 November 2003.

About to exit the north end of Arpley yard to reach the stabling point on 9 July 1973 is 7639 (25289) from Springs Branch.

On 5 January 1975 25298 from Springs Branch is stabled at Ladywell, Preston.

A train composed of five Brake vans approaches Wakefield Kirkgate on the line from Normanton on 3 January 1975. It is headed by Spring Branch's 25300.

Mid-evening on weekdays at St.Austell in the mid-seventies saw three trains meet and re-marshall in the station area. On 1 August 1974 the operation has been completed and 25306 departs westwards with a freight while 46024 waits in the small yard to depart eastwards with another freight. The 25 was allocated to Laira and the 46 to Bath Road.

Exeter depot held Laira's 7657 (25307) and Newton Abbot's 4160 (08930) on 12 September 1971.

On 3 July 1974 25318 from Springs Branch awaits it next duty at Northwich shed.

Inside Barrow shed on 13 October 1974 were 25320 from Kingmoor and the shed's own 08922.

Here is D7672 (25322) 'TAMWORTH CASTLE' at Stockport on 27 October 1990. This engine was withdrawn in January 1984, but was named and re-instated in May of that year as 25912. It was withdrawn again in March 1987 and after storage for a while was transferred to Departmental stock in April 1987. It should have been re-numbered to ADB 968027 but this did not take place. In November 1990 it was re-instated to revenue stock as 25912 but continued to carry D7672 as seen in the photo. Following withdrawal in March 1991 it operates from Cheddleton on the preserved North Staffordshire Railway.

Working an Engineer's train to Cheddleton D7672 (25322) approaches Consall Forge level crossing on 17 August 1997.

A line of engines at Canton depot on 12 August 1972 include 1934 (47256), 7675 (25325) and 7516 (25166). The last loco was allocated to Ebbw Junction, Newport.

A Down Parcels train at Exeter St.Davids on 29 March 1975 is headed by Laira's 25326

It is mid-evening at St.Austell on 1 August 1974 as 25326 departs with an Up freight and 25306 waits in the short refuge siding. Both were Laira engines. The Western National Bus Garage is prominent upper left. This building was St.Austell's awkwardly placed second Goods shed which was accessed by a back shunt over a level crossing from the Down main line. The level crossing, which was on a steep hill was replaced by a footbridge, the grey top of which appears just above the top of the station footbridge. The road footbridge was originally at St.Blazey station.

Three class 25s after withdrawal were utilised to heat trains. They were named ETHELs which stood for Electric Train Heating Unit Ex Locomotive. On 27 August 1984 25305 in the guise of 97251 'ETHEL 2' is warming carriages at Fort William. This engine was allocated to Eastfield and carries the depot's Scotty dog emblem. After conversion it was allotted the number ADB968025 but this was never carried.

97252 'ETHEL 3' was originally 25314. The allocated number ADB 968026 was never carried. On 23 March 1987 this Bletchley allocated loco was at Marylebone depot where I was granted permission to photograph it. The engine was in a very awkward and inaccessible spot.

CLASSES 26 and 27
DIESEL LOCOMOTIVES

By the time I really caught up with these types of locomotives they were all based in Scotland, but strangely I did see 27008 at Didcot in April 1976. Some of them have strayed south in preservation.

CLASS 26s

Carrying a plaque bearing Eastfield's Scottie dog emblem 26003 is inside Grangemouth shed on 17 May 1992.

The east end of Millerhill depot was viewed from a diverted HST on 25 October 1987. Left to right are 47085 from Cardiff Canton, 47218 from Crewe Diesel, 37008 from Tinsley and Haymarket's 26006.

On the preserved Caledonian Railway at Bridge of Dun on 4 August 2002 26014 is at the west end of the station.

The last train of the day from Bridge of Dun on 4 August 2002 was banked in the rear by 26014. It is approaching the train over the foot crossing to couple up. I was treated to a cab ride to Brechin on this loco.

A line of engines inside Inverness depot on 2 June 1976 contained 26015.

Eastfield's 26015 was on an Engineer's train in Rutherglen Permanent Way yard on 27 August 1988.

Two Inverness engines are at Wick on 3 June 1976. 26019 waits in a siding with a short freight whilst 26027 is sandwiched between several carriages.

Two Inverness engines are about to pass at Georgemas Junction on 3 June 1976. At the platform 26020 has arrived from Thurso as 26027 approaches the overline bridge with a train from Wick.

On 3 June 1976 Inverness's 26020 waits to depart from Thurso with a train to Georgemas Junction. The station retained a short overall roof.

Centrepiece at Ferryhill depot on 2 June 1976 is 26023 from Inverness. The cab of another Inverness engine 26028 can be seen behind the Brake van on the right. Inside road no. 2 on the left is 47433 from York depot.

Inverness depot's 26027 waits to cross another train at Helmsdale with a train from Inverness to Wick on 3 June 1976. The mountains creep down to the lineside.

On 3 June 1976 26027 from Inverness has arrived at Wick and is partly under the short overall roof buffered up to a coach already present.

A surprise was to find 26028 and 26036 from Eastfield at Carlisle on 13 July 1991. The two engines provided a contrast in liveries.

On 26 August 1985 47106 from Tinsley and 26029 from Haymarket were at the south end of Dundee station.

On 8 June 1976 Inverness depot's 26030 awaits departure from Kyle of Lochalsh.

We look east out of Kyle of Lochalsh on 8 June 1976 as 26030 from Inverness waits to depart. The signal box is in the distance by the next overline bridge.

Two trains are crossing at Achnasheen in the evening on 8 June 1976. 26032 is approaching on a train to Kyle of Lochalsh. 26030 waits to proceed towards Inverness where both engines were allocated.

Two trains are crossing at Brora on 3 June 1976. 26033 is approaching with a train to Wick. 26027 waits to proceed to Inverness where both engines were based.

Three engines are lined up outside part of Haymarket depot on 25 September 1982. On the left is 26034 from Inverness. Centre is 20216 with 27010 on the right.

Perth station on 31 August 1983 with Inverness depot's 26034 on the short 17.10 to Dundee and Arbroath. Despite it being summer the engine is fitted with snow ploughs.

Stabled at Bridge of Dun on the Caledonian Railway on 4 August 2002 are preserved 26035 and 26014.

At Dalwhinnie with an Engineer's train on 31 August 1983 is 26037 from Haymarket.

On 10 August 1997 26038 is at the South Yorkshire Railway at Meadowhall.

On 23 August 1984 26039 was moving around the yard at Inverness depot. This engine is also fitted with snow ploughs.

Recorded from Stirling station footbridge on 2 December 1987 Eastfield's 26040 was in the adjacent yard.

On 27 August 1988 26040 from Eastfield, in Railfreight grey livery was at Ayr depot.

On 3 August 1991 Eastfield's 26041, carrying the depot's Scottie dog emblem is at Carlisle with a Branch Line Society special train.

On 23 August 1992 Perth station locomotive holding sidings held 26042 and 08762 both of which were Inverness engines.

Inside Inverness depot in a line of engines on 2 June 1976 is 26043.

This is 26043 in Inverness depot on 2 June 1976 seen from the opposite end.

Haymarket's 26046 is stabled at Perth station with two tank wagons on 26 August 1985.

CLASS 27s

Trains cross at Bridge of Orchy on 7 June 1976. Eastfield's 27001 waits with a train from Mallaig to Glasgow Queen Street as a Mallaig bound train enters the station. On the right is the remnants of the small yard with exit signal and trap point.

Across the main lines opposite Polmadie depot a stabling point was established at Shawfield sidings. On 27 August 1985 one of the occupants was Eastfield's 27002.

On 17 May 1992 hemmed in by other engines at Bo'ness was preserved 27005. The 0-4-0ST masquerading as NCB no.42 is ex LNER Y9 class 68095.

In the yard at Eastfield depot on 5 June 1976 is 27014.

In one of the Bay platforms at the Up end of Dundee station on 6 September 1983 is Haymarket's 27017. The train is the 15.21 to Edinburgh Waverley.

On 8 June 1976 Eastfield's 27018 waits at Fort William with a train to Mallaig.

The train from Fort William hauled by 27018 from Eastfield depot has arrived at Mallaig on 8 June 1976 and has disgorged passengers, many of whom are possibly heading for Skye.

With a mountain as a backdrop, Eastfield's 27020 waits at Crianlarich Upper with a train to Glasgow Queen Street on 7 June 1976. A train from Glasgow to Oban has arrived at the platform.

On 7 June 1976 Eastfield's 27023
departs from Oban with a train to
Glasgow Queen Street.

Preserved 27024 is stored on one of the
platform lines at Bridge of Dun on the
Caledonian Railway on 4 August 2002.
To its left is 350hp shunter D3059
(08046).

With the castle prominent above, 27029 from Eastfield is at the buffers at Oban after arrival from Glasgow Street on 7 June 1976. So many passengers detrained here that I had to exercise patience to obtain a clear shot of the engine.

Corkerhill depot was photographed from the 14.01 Kilmacolm to Glasgow Central on 8 January 1983. This was the last day of public passengers services on the Kilmacolm branch. From left to right the engines are 47274 from Haymarket, and 27034 and 47163 both from Eastfield.

On 7 June 1976 a train from Glasgow Queen Street to Oban in charge of 27044 from Eastfield awaits departure from Arrochar and Tarbet. Mountains tower upper right in the distance.

Resting inside Inverness depot on 23 August 1984 arc 27053 and 27051. These engines had previously been numbered 27109 and 27107.

Two trains wait to depart from Glasgow Queen Street on 1 September 1983. On the left is 37112 which later became 37510. To the right 27055 (ex 27111) is on the 16.50 to Dundee. Both engines were based at Eastfield

In preservation engines appear at locations many miles distant from their former spheres of operation. This classic example has 27066 (ex 27212 and 27103) and Southern Region ED E6001 (73001) in the yard by the diesel depot at Lydney Junction on the Dean Forest Railway on 4 September 2007.

The old station and Goods depot at Stranraer Town were used for stabling stock and locomotives. On 30 August 1983 Eastfield's 27101 waits in the yard on what appears to be Sleeper stock. This engine later became 27045.

Three locomotives are in Stranraer Town yard on 30 August 1983. Furthest left is 27101 (later 27045). Centre is 27211 which had been 27117 and became 27065. Nearest the camera is 47408. These engines were allocated to Eastfield, Haymarket and Gateshead.

With a mountain in the distance two Eastfield engines are on trains crossing at Glen Douglas on 7 June 1976. 27029 is on a train from Glasgow Queen Street to Oban. Waiting to depart alongside the signal box is 27105 which later became 27049. For many years a small halt for passengers existed at this location.

The driver stands in the cab doorway of Eastfield's 27105 (27049) as it waits at Glen Douglas with a Glasgow bound freight train on 7 June 1976.

Shunting in the yard at the south end of Montrose station on 26 August 1985 is Eastfield's 27207 which had previously been numbered 27113. Due to have become 27061 it was withdrawn before this number was applied but was taken into Departmental stock and numbered to supposedly ADB 968025. However this was erroneously applied as ADB68025. Passing on a southbound train is 47463 from Crewe Diesel.

Stabled on passenger stock in Stranraer Town yard on 30 August 1983 is 27211 from Haymarket depot. This engine had previously been numbered 27117 and later became 27065.

CLASS 40, 44, 45 and 46 DIESEL LOCOMOTIVES

Class 40s worked form London to the east and north and into Wales. Class 44s mainly stayed around the East Midlands. Class 45s and 46s penetrated to most areas apart form the south of England.

CLASS 40s

A train from Carlisle to Leeds calls at Skipton on 9 September 1983. It is headed by 40004 from Longsight depot.

This is another view of Longsight's 40004 at Skipton on 9 September 1983.

On 29 June 1974 40013 from Longsight waits to depart from Llandudno with a train to Manchester.

Keeping company with DMUs at Buxton depot on 25 April 1977 is the same engine 40013.

Again we see 40013, this time at Carlisle heading the 16.35 to Leeds on 7 September 1983. The engine had moved to Crewe Diesel.

This is Buxton depot on 15 March 1977. Left is 40004 with 40019 centre. Peeping out of the shed is 46023. These engines were based at Longsight, Springs Branch and Cardiff Canton.

On 26 April 1977 40019 was on Springs Branch depot coupled to the Breakdown crane.

Holyhead used the old steam shed as a diesel depot. Photography there was somewhat difficult on 16 May 1980 due to glaring sun. Stabled in the shed on that day are 40024 from Longsight and 08746.

Outside Northwich shed on 2 July 1973 is 225 (40025) from Longsight depot.

Rounding the curve from Crofton into Wakefield Kirkgate on 3 January 1975 is 40036 which was a Healey Mills engine.

On 6 January 1975 Healey Mills's 40036 again passed through Wakefield Kirkgate.

On 3 January 1975 40040 from Healey Mills passes through Wakefield Kirkgate.

Healey Mills's 40040 passes east through Wakefield Kirkgate on a freight on 6 January 1975.

A train being unloaded in the yard at
Rose Grove on 8 July 1974 is headed
by 40051 which was based at Healey
Mills.

York's 40081 waits to depart eastwards
with a passenger train from Leeds on 3
January 1975.

Keeping company with a class 47 in the stabling bays at Preston on 6 July 1974 was 40082 from Springs Branch.

On 3 June 1976 the stabling shed at Inverness depot was full. Partly outside is 40083 from York depot. Visible inside on the right is 26017.

Stabled in the yard at Springs Branch on 26 April 1977 is Kingmoor's 40088.

Rounding the east curve out of the large marshalling yard at Arpley, Warrington on 9 July 1973 is 303 (40103) from Longsight.

Three class 40s are stabled at Springs Branch on 26 April 1977. Front left is 40106 from Longsight still retaining its headcode box. 40179 to its rear is from Kingmoor. On the right is 40019.

Longsight's 40114 sits outside Northwich shed on 3 July 1974.

Stabled at Buxton depot on 25 April 1977 is Longsight's 40116.

Outside the depot at Longsight on 24 April 1977 is 40117.

Buxton depot on 25 April 1977 has Longsight's 40121 outside.

On 8 September 1983. 40122 (D200) enters Settle with a train from Carlisle to Leeds. The engine was based at Kingmoor.

On a very wet 8 September 1983 green liveried 40122 (D200) from Kingmoor rounds the curve on the approach to Skipton with a Leeds to Carlisle working.

On 1 June 1984 Kingmoor's 40122 (D200) in green livery waits with stock on the centre road at Sheffield Midland.

In the evening of 5 July 1974 a pair of class 40s were stabled at Dam Bridge sidings, Garston, Liverpool. Left retaining headcode twin boxes is 40125 with 40079 nearest to the camera. Both engines were allocated to Springs Branch.

Three diesels are stabled north of the station at Bury on the East Lancashire Railway on 25 November 1990. They are 40145, D1041 'WESTERN PRINCE' and D335 (40135).

Several engines are lined up in the holding sidings at Finsbury Park depot on 25 June 1978. They are 40146 from Thornaby and 31125 which has 37098 from Healey Mills to its rear. A 'Deltic' is in background.

Gateshead's 40150 eases past Leeds on 3 January 1975.

The holding sidings at Finsbury Park depot contained numerous engines on 25 June 1978. They are 37098, 40159 and 40146. These engines were allocated to Healey Mills, Haymarket and Thornaby.

Stored in the yard at Haymarket depot on 6 September 1983 are 20215 and withdrawn 40162 (D62).

Displaying its
headcode numbers
40156 from Healey
Mills brings an
eastbound freight
through Wakefield
Kirkgate on 6 January
1975.

A view of Northwich
shed on 30 May
1976. Inside are
08689 from Allerton,
25209 from Longsight
and 40185. Outside
is 40171. Both class
40s were Spring
Branch engines.

This is part of the yard at Springs Branch depot on 26 April 1977. In the foreground is 40179. Far right are 25289 and Longsight's 25209.

On 3 January 1975 40182 from Springs Branch moves a train of tank wagons past Leeds.

A train of hopper wagons from one of the yards at Bidston approaching a level crossing on 9 July 1973 is headed by 384 (40184) from Springs Branch depot.

Standing in Sheffield Midland station on 17 June 1978 is 40193 from Healey Mills depot.

The stabling sidings at Blackburn on 13 March 1977 held 40195 from Healey Mills which is partly hiding 40125 from Springs Branch.

Healey Mills's 40195 and Spring Branch's 40125 are viewed from a different angle at Blackburn on 13 March 1977. The pair offer a contrast in headcode boxes.

Taken against the light on 16 October 1976 44002 is outside one of the servicing sheds at Toton depot.

On 23 April 1977 the North West branch of the Locomotive Club of Great Britain ran their 'CLASS 44 Peak' railtour. The train headed by 44004 stopped at Hinckley for pathing and photographic purposes. This loco has been preserved at the Midland Railway Centre.

On 16 October 1976 44005 stands in the yard at the north end of Toton depot.

Lady Luck also played her hand when I was at Leicester on 2 January 1976 as 44010 passed through the station. I was not in an at all ideal position but nonetheless I managed to record it. The loco only carried 44 on each end of the side seen but a local enthusiast who was 'in the know' identified it for me.

With too many obstacles in the way to obtain a perfect shot it was a case of 'beggars can't be choosers' when Tinsley's 45009 brought a short freight into Par heading for St.Blazey yard on 21 September 1984.

Three engines are lined up outside Exeter depot on 28 February 1971. Left to right they are Warship class 849 ''SUPERB' and class 22 6330 both from Newton Abbot depot. On the right is 17 (45024) from Holbeck.

This is a distant view of engines lined up at the back of Gateshead depot on 30 September 1975 taken form a train crossing the King Edward Bridge. Against the shed door is shunter 00044 Lined up on the right are 47145, 45060 in the centre and 47245. These three were allocated to Bescot, Cricklewood and Cardiff Canton.

Preserved at Peak Rail at Matlock on 25 June 1988 is D100 (45060).

A train pulls away from Plymouth on 28 February 1976 past the closed North Road East signal box headed by 45072 from Cricklewood depot. The train is about to pass shunter 08643.

A local DMU to Par passes 45105 on a train from Manchester Piccadilly to Newquay at Goonbarrow Junction on 16 June 1984. The Peak was allocated to Toton.

A train bound for Newcastle Central passes Ferryhill South Junction on 9 June 1984. The train is headed by Toton's 45115.

On 3 January 1975 45126 from Toton runs west past Leeds.

A special train organised by The Locomotive Club of Great Britain on 1 November 1986 waits at Swanwick Junction prior to departure for Butterley. It is headed by 'Deltic' 9015 'TULYAR' and Peak 45127.

An 'Open Day' was held at Laira depot on 15 September 1991. To the fore is 'Deltic' 55015 'TULYAR'. To the rear of that loco is Peak 45133. On the right is 08645. A class 50 is in the distance.

CLASS 46s

Two trains wait at St.Austell in the evening of 1 August 1974. In the main platform the Up Postal is headed by Laira's D1066 'WESTERN PREFECT'. In the yard on a fitted freight is Bath Road's 46024.

An 'Open Day' for family and friends was held by EWS at St.Blazey depot on 31 August 2002. Many visiting engines were present. On the left is Peak 46035 with 50042 'TRIUMPH' on the right which operates on the Bodmin & Wenford Railway.

CLASS 31 DIESEL and 76 and 77 ELECTRIC LOCOMOTIVES

A loco at a depot with no allocation quoted means the loco is at home. Any images not taken by myself are credited with the photographers name if known.

Class 76 and 77 locos worked on the electrified Woodhead route between Manchester, Sheffield and Wath. The class 31s sphere of operation was far more widespread and in later years they have appeared much further afield..

CLASS 31s

A line of engines at Stratford depot on 22 March 1980 contained 31004.

Stratford depot contained many class 31s on 24 June 1978. This line up includes 31019, 31005 and 31122. Two of them have the well known white roofs which was a hallmark of Stratford depot.

On 22 March 1980 a long line of class 31s at Stratford included 31017.

Also at Stratford on 22 March 1980 are white roofed 31019 and 31103.

In Fragonset Railways livery 31106 'SPALDING TOWN' runs past Wakefield Kirkgate on 24 June 2002.

Preserved 31108 rests at Wansford on the Nene Valley Railway on 22 June 2002.

Most unusually on 3 December 1987 31130 from Crewe Diesel was alongside the small shed at Taunton.

Against the buffers at Paddington on 17 August 1988 is 31132 from Tinsley depot.

On 13 August 1988 passengers at Norwich are boarding the 10.20 to Yarmouth which is headed by Tinsley's 31142.

Tinsley's 31142 is ready to depart from Yarmouth Vauxhall with the 17.11 to Norwich on 13 August 1988.

A contrast in liveries is presented by 31142 and 31201 as they bring an Engineers train southwards through Crewe on 29 April 1996. Both engines were allocated to Springs Branch depot.

The yard at York depot on 13 April 1975 held 31147 along with 31211 and 31314 which were both allocated to March.

The stabling point at Peak Forest contained Snow Plough ADB 965308 on 26 April 1996. To the rear of the Snow Plough is 31159 from Springs Branch which sustained damage when it collided with a Permanent Way vehicle here on 4 April.

On 22 April 1996 31163 from Springs Branch brings a short freight train around the curve into Arpley yard, Warrington. Visible centre right is 56127 from Cardiff Canton which is waiting a path into the yard from the stabling point.

A short Engineers train heads south through Warrington Bank Quay on 25 April1996 headed by 31166 from Bescot depot.

An Overhead Wiring train, seen from a train on the Docklands Light Railway is at Carpenters Road West Junction on 12 June 1988. It is hauled by Stratford's 31173.

Among engines stabled at Arpley, Warrington on 25 April 1996 is 31201 from Springs Branch.

An Open Day was held at Doncaster Works on 17 June 1978 when one of the locos on display was 31208 from March depot.

Photographed from inside a Leeds bound DMU on 14 October 1974 the yard south of Skipton station contained a short freight in charge of March depot's 31213. This loco was renumbered to 31465.

Contrasting liveries are carried by 31275 and 31233 ' SEVERN VALLEY RAILWAY' which are on Arpley stabling point on 23 April 1996. These engines were allocated to Springs Branch and Crewe Diesel.

17 July 2002 was a non-operating day at the Colne Valley Railway. In the extensive yard carrying EWS livery but devoid of any readily visual identification is 31255.

Among various items of stock on 17 July 2002 at the Colne Valley Railway is 31270.

Stabled at Old Oak Common depot on 24 June 1978 is 31273.

During a Diesel Gala on the Bodmin & Wenford Railway on 21 September 1997 visiting 31273 awaits departure from Bodmin General. This engine was based at Crewe Diesel but had been transferred 'on paper' to Bescot. Class 31s were rare visitors to Cornwall at this time.

During a Diesel Gala on the Bodmin & Wenford Railway on 21 September 1997 Crewe Diesel's 31273 waits at Bodmin Parkway with a train for Bodmin General.

On 14 June 1983 Immingham's 31279 heads north past Chesterfield with a train of coal hoppers. Later this engine became 31452.

During engineering works in the area on 15 February 1984 several trains were stabled at Sheffield Midland. One of these is headed by 31280 and 37013 which were allocated to Bescot and Tinsley.

Visits to Gateshead depot were rarely permitted. On the evening of 1 April 1989 I was lucky to be allowed entry and was conducted around the establishment by a driver. On the left inside the 'Day shed' with coupling rods removed are withdrawn 08608 and 08671. Centre with a large format number is Thornaby's 31281 which was withdrawn from service six weeks later.

In Network Rail livery 31285 was a rare visitor to Cornwall on 20 September 2005 when it is passing west through St.Austell en route to Penzance in the morning.

Returning from Penzance on 20 September 2005 Network Rail's 31285 visited Newquay before proceeding east. It is approaching Middleway Bridge level crossing on the return run early in the evening.

Gateshead's 31288 shunts loaded coal hoppers into the yard at Hexham on 6 April 1979.

Three class 31s are passing through Middlesborough on 16 April 1975. Left of centre 31292 slowly moves a train of loaded bogie flats westwards. Approaching at speed with a train of empty wagons are 31130 and 31276. The large docks complex form a backdrop. The last mentioned loco was from Tinsley and the others were from nearby Thornaby.

This is a distant view of Marylebone depot from the end of the station platforms on 24 March 1987. The three engines visible are 08556, Bescot's 31294 and 'ETHEL 3' (ex 97252 and 25314).

Several locos are stabled at Gloucester Horton Road depot on 12 August 1972. Left to right they comprise 5213 (25063), 5828 (31295), 5227 (25077) and 1611 (47032). The 25s and 31 were Bath Road engines and the 47 was from Landore.

Harry Needle stored engines which he had acquired at various locations one of which was Meldon Quarry. Here on 3 September 2004 47348, 31301 and 73103 can be seen along with the upper part of 08937. Two parallel lines of engines made identification difficult.

Around one of the turntables at Old Oak Common on 24 June 1978 are 31304 carrying the bodyline white stripe and 08787.

On 3 December 1977 the stabling point at Kings Cross was host to Finsbury Park's 31407 and Haymarkets 47272.

Stabled at Arpley on 25 April 1996 is Spring Branch's 31410 'GRANADA TELETHON'.

Gateshead's 31411 waits on stock at Newcastle Central on 12 April 1975.

On 1 June 1984 31411, now an Immingham engine, waits on empty coaching stock at Sheffield Midland. This engine subsequently became 31511 and then reverted to 31411.

Among Harry Needle's class 31s stored at Meldon Quarry on 8 May 2005 were 31415 and 31426.

Two locomotive hauled trains await departure from Scarborough Central on 27 May 1972. They are headed by York's 5522 (31418) and Tinsley's 6790 (37090). A good display of semaphore signals is evident.

To my surprise a train for Manchester Piccadilly arrived at Stafford in the morning of 9 August 1997 hauled by a pair of class 31s. The engines are Bescot's 31420 (ex 31172) and 31434 (ex 312 8).

Stored at Meldon Quarry on 3 September 2004 are Harry Needle's 31423 (ex 31197), 31439 (ex 31239) and 47348.

On 18 October 1989 Bescot's 31424 has arrived at Lincoln Central on a passenger working. It had previously carried 31157 and was again renumbered to 31524. Later it was officially renumbered back to 31424 but continued to carry 31524.

Among Harry Needle's engine stored at Meldon Quarry on 8 May 2005 are 31426 (ex 31193, later 31526, then back to 31426) and 31437.

Another shot of Harry Needle's engines at Meldon Quarry on 8 May 2005 has 31437 (ex 31182, later 31537, then back to 31437) and 73103.

Immingham's 31439 (ex 31239) is running round its train after arrival at Cleethorpes on 12 September 1985.

By now sold to Harry Needle 31439 (ex 31239) along with 31423 is stored at Meldon Quarry on 3 September 2004.

This is the scene at Sheffield Midland when an Open Day was held at Tinsley depot on 27 April 1996. On a special working is Ferrybridge depot's 59205. Also present for railtour duty are Bescot's 31462 (ex 31315, later 31562, then back to 31462) and 31468 (ex 31321, later 31568, then back to 31468).

On 10 July 1985 Immingham's 31463 (ex 31297 and later 31563) waits to depart from Manchester Piccadilly with a train to Cleethorpes.

In a most inaccessible position and partly obscured by a crane 31466 (ex 31115) is in a line of engines outside the Dean Forest Railway's diesel depot at Lydney Junction on 4 September 2007. To its rear is 27008.

This is the scene at Kings Lynn during the West Anglia Gala Day on 29 September 1990. Far left partly hidden is 45133. At the platform are Cardiff Canton's 37711 'TREMORFA STEELWORKS' and 31541 (ex 31220 and 31441) from Immingham. In the distance to the right of centre are Southern Region EDs 73129 and 73103 which were very rare visitors.

We end with a pair of Fragonset Railways class 31s at Newton Abbot on 14 May 2000 during a two day Festival of Transport in the town. On a special working are 31601 'BLETCHLEY PARK STATION' (ex 31186) and 31602 'CHIMAERA' (ex 31191).

CLASS 76

To save repetition, when photographed all of these locos were working from Reddish depot. They were also stabled at Darnall and Wath depots and stabling points existed at Dewsnap yard and Rotherwood holding sidings.

Several of the class alongside Reddish depot on 24 April 1977 include 76004 and 76053.

A line of the class at Wath depot on 1 March 1975 include 76024, 76013, 76027.

Also at Wath on 1 March 1975 were 76016, 76015 and 76004.

The same line of engines at Wath on 1 March 1975 viewed from the other direction contained 76015, 76016, 76004 and 76053.

The sole example that has been preserved is 26020 (76020). This is inside the National Railway Museum at York in the 1990s. Maurice Dart collection.

Two more of the class at Wath on 1 March 1975 are 76024 and 76013.

Another line of engines at Reddish on 24 April 1977 consist of Newton Heath's 08676 with 76048 (ex 76039) and 76002.

On 1 March 1975 76056 had its pantograph raised and was on the move at Wath.

All seven of these engines were sold to Netherlands Railways and two have returned home. Carrying its Dutch number of 1502, the original 27000 is in the shed at Swanwick Junction on 1 November 1986.

On display at Tinsley depot on the Open day on 27 April 1996, the same loco has been repainted, renumbered to E27000 and renamed 'ELECTRA'.

INDEX

CLASSES 26 and 27 DIESEL LOCOMOTIVES

CLASS 40, 44, 45 and 46 DIESEL LOCOMOTIVES

CLASS 31 DIESEL and 76 and 77 ELECTRIC LOCOMOTIVES